DATING A
WIDWER

DATING A
WID⬤WER

STARTING A RELATIONSHIP
WITH A MAN
WHO'S STARTING OVER

ABEL KEOGH

BEN LOMOND
PRESS

Published by
Ben Lomond Press
Copyright © 2011 by Abel Keogh
All rights reserved

Cover design by Francine Eden Platt of Eden Graphics, Inc.
Cover design Copyright © 2011 by Abel Keogh

This is a self-help book. Opinions expressed are those of the author.
ISBN 10: 0615528392
ISBN 13: 978-0615528397

TABLE OF CONTENTS

INTRODUCTION:

WHY I WROTE
DATING A WIDOWER

YOU'VE MET A MAN that knocks you off your feet. Everything about him is perfect except for one thing: He's a widower. And that makes you pause. Is he ready to move on and start a new life with me? Has he finished grieving? If the relationship works out, will he love me as much as the late wife? These and a thousand other questions go through your head. Well, you're in luck.

The purpose of this book isn't to discourage you from dating a widower. Rather, it's to 1) give you insight into the heart and mind of a widower so you can better understand his behavior and 2) help you decide for yourself if the widower you're dating is ready to start a new life with you, or whether he's just looking to fill the hole in his heart.

As a widower who has since remarried, I've seen too many men (myself included) start dating before they're emotionally ready to make serious commitments to the women they claim to love. I've also corresponded with hundreds of women who have fallen in love with men who claimed to be ready to move on but, in the end, were not. Most of these women could have avoided heartache if they'd been aware of the red flags.

The good news is that there are many widowers out there who are ready to make room in their heart for another person. As I write this, I've been married to Julianna for eight years. I also personally know many other widowers who are happily remarried. We know how fortunate and blessed we are to have someone with whom we can spend the rest of our lives.

I hope the widower you're dating is one of those men.

Abel Keogh

August 2011

CHAPTER 1

WIDOWERS— THEY'RE STILL MEN!

WIDOWERS ARE MEN. It doesn't matter how long they were married, how their wife died, or how long it's been since their wife passed on—widowers act, think, and grieve like men. There are no widower issues— only man issues.

When you think of widowers as men, you can better understand the motivations and reasons behind their actions and decide for yourself whether he's ready to move on and start a new life with you, or simply looking to fill the hole in his heart or for someone to warm his bed at night.

When it comes to men, there are five things you

need to know about them that affects their behavior after they've lost a spouse.

1. WIDOWERS HAVE AN INTERNAL NEED FOR RELATIONSHIPS

A few weeks after my late wife, Krista, and I were married, we had dinner with her grandmother, a widow. During dinner, her grandmother told us that a neighbor and good friend had recently passed away after a long illness. After we expressed our condolences, her grandmother told us how the woman's husband had stopped by to invite her to the funeral. After she told the man she planned on coming, the man had then told Krista's grandmother he'd be calling on her soon.

Krista and I were floored. How could anyone even think about dating someone else when their wife wasn't even buried yet? On the way home from dinner that night, I told Krista that if she died, I'd never remarry. Krista gave my arm a squeeze and told me she felt the same way.

Two years after that conversion, Krista committed suicide. In the months following her death, I found myself wanting to date again. I felt guilty for having these feelings. I thought there was something wrong with me; perhaps I was angry at Krista about taking her own life, and as a result, I was trying to get even with her. But the desire to date again grew stronger with each passing day. Finally, I gave in to the feelings and signed up with an online dating site and went on my first widower date a few weeks later. Later I met a wonderful woman named Julianna. We fell in love and were married 15 months after Krista died. (As I write this, we're a month shy of celebrating our eighth anniversary.)

It wasn't until after I remarried and started researching how men grieve that I realized my desire to date again so soon after Krista's death was natural. After losing a spouse, most widowers find that the richness and purpose life once held is gone. Their life feels broken, and they want to fix it. *The most logical way to do that? Find another woman.* And while there's nothing wrong with dating months or weeks after a spouse dies, most widowers who start dating again are still grieving the loss of their spouse. They're not emotionally ready to make long-term or serious commitments to the women they're dating.

Unfortunately, this doesn't stop widowers from telling the women they're dating that they love them and are ready to start a new life. A lot of women end up falling in love with a widower, only to end up with a broken heart after the widower unexpectedly tells her he's not ready to move on.

2. WIDOWERS WILL STAY IN RELATIONSHIPS WITH WOMEN THEY DON'T LOVE

Because widowers have a strong desire to be in a relationship, they will get serious with women they don't really love. Most widowers are just happy to have a woman in their life again. Often, their loneliness is so acute that they'll attach themselves to the first person who shows the slightest interest in them. Having someone who will hold them and tell them how much they're needed or loved will overcome the nagging feeling in the back of their mind that the relationship isn't right—at least for a while.

Sometimes it's hard to tell which men are serious about moving on and which are just looking for someone to lessen the ache in their hearts. Both types of widowers will treat you like a queen, tell you how much they love you, and do other things that make you feel like the center of their universe. However, widowers who aren't serious about starting over with you can only fake these relationships for so long. Sooner or later, the doubts that have been nagging them since they first became serious with you will overwhelm their desire for companionship. Once they reach that point, those widowers who still have a shred of manliness in them will tell you the relationship isn't working out and end it.

Soon after I started dating, I became serious with a woman I'll call Jennifer. We were friends before I was married to Krista, and after her death, we reconnected. I flirted with her, started dating her, and eventually told her I wanted to spend the rest of my life with her. During our relationship, I never loved Jennifer—at least, not in the way you need to love someone to spend the rest of your life with him or her. When we were together, I couldn't see myself marrying or having a family with her. Despite these reservations, I didn't want to lose her. Having Jennifer in my life brought a sense of normalcy that had been missing since Krista died. Having someone at my side was better than having no one. Eventually I ended the relationship, but it came at a high price. I lost a good friend, and Jennifer ended up with a broken heart and confused feelings.

If you want to avoid giving your heart to a man who's not ready to move on, my advice is to take things slowly—especially in the first few months of the relationship. It's also a good way to learn if the widower is looking for a long-term relationship or looking to fill the hole in his heart. A widower who sees a potential long-term, committed relationship with you will be fine taking things slow. He'll patiently wait for you to be ready while finding ways to prove his feelings for you. If he's just looking for sex, companionship, or a therapist, he'll push you to speed things up, threaten to date other people, or quickly lose interest in the relationship.

When a relationship is new and they guy seems like a great catch, it's very easy to get emotionally swept up in the moment and overlook possible warning signs that he's not ready to open his heart to you. However, taking things slow when it comes to physical or emotional intimacy is a small price to pay in order to avoid getting your heart crushed.

3. Widowers Pursue Women They're Interested In

Men, by nature, are pursuers. When the right woman catches their eye, they'll do just about anything and everything they can to show the woman how much they love them.

The same is true for widowers. When widowers find someone they truly love, they'll put aside the grief and make you the number one person in their hearts and minds. Widowers who are ready to move on will voluntarily take down photos of the late wife, remove the wedding ring, and make you feel like the only woman he's ever loved. Nothing will stop them from starting a new life with someone else—including their grief. It may not happen overnight, but you'll see steady progress from the widower and have little doubt that he's making room in his heart for you.

The best way to tell if a man is interested in pursuing you is to give him a chance to take the lead in the relationship. Let him plan dates and other activities, and let him initiate most of the communication. Doing this accomplishes two things. First, it forces the widower to decide how serious he is about you. A man who has doubts about the relationship will eventually grow tired of having to prove his love to someone when he isn't really interested. Eventually he'll end it.

Second, this helps him make room in his heart for you. Widowers prove their love through actions and sacrifice. The more they can prove their love through actions, the easier it is for them to develop the deep love needed to put their grief aside and start a new life. Without this deep love, it's extremely difficult for him to make room in his heart for you.

I want to make one thing clear: There's nothing wrong with setting up dates or calling him. I'm not saying you have to let him initiate *everything*. But if you find yourself doing most of the heavy lifting in the relationship, it's easy for him to simply go along for the ride instead of deciding if the relationship is right for him.

There's a part of me that believes I never would have gotten serious with Jennifer had she let me take more of the lead when we started dating. Because of the doubts in the back of my mind, I hesitated to set up dates and other activities once it became clear that there was a mutual interest in taking things forward. Jennifer, however, had no problem taking the lead. And I had no problem letting her. After all, it felt nice to have someone who wanted to be at my side as often as possible. All I had to do was tell her that I loved her and wanted to spend the rest of my life with her. I never really had to prove those feelings because Jennifer was eager to take charge.

Julianna, on the other hand, behaved in the opposite way. In addition to having a somewhat shy personality, she also had a lot of concerns about dating a widower and was hesitant to get involved with someone whose late wife had only been dead six months. It quickly became obvious that the only chance I had at winning her heart was to prove to her that I was ready to make her number one in my heart. It took about three months of dating before she felt comfortable becoming serious with me. During that time, I did everything I could to show her that I was ready to start a new life with her. And in the end, I not only proved my love to her, but proved to myself that I could heal from the loss of a spouse, open my heart to someone else, and love that person just as much.

4.   MEN CAN ONLY ACTIVELY LOVE ONE WOMAN AT A TIME

Most women wouldn't get involved with a divorced man who was still angry and bitter toward an ex-wife or a single man who was still anguishing over a failed romance. Yet many women will fall in love with a widower who's still mourning for his late spouse. These women usually believe that if they're patient and are there for him while he grieves, he'll eventually move on.

Nothing could be further from the truth. While the human heart has a great capacity for love, widowers can only actively love one woman at a time. It doesn't matter if the woman is alive or dead; they can only devote their thoughts, feelings, and attention to one woman. If they're constantly thinking about the late wife, they won't be able to do what it takes to move on and love someone else.

In order to move on, widowers need to focus their time, energy, and attention on you, instead of the late wife. This means that their utmost thoughts and feelings are on you and your happiness, and not on how much they miss the dead spouse. Widowers who are truly ready for a long-term, committed relationship won't have a problem taking this step.

Some widowers can give you their full attention for a short time. For example, when I dated Jennifer, I was able to focus my attention and thoughts on her when we were together. However, when I wasn't in her presence or talking to her, my thoughts quickly returned to Krista and the life we had together. As a result, I was never able to find a place in my heart for Jennifer.

I didn't have that problem with Julianna. In fact, I couldn't get her out of my mind. My thoughts and attention were always focused on her and her happiness. Because I was so focused on Julianna, I became less and less focused on my loss. This made it easier for me to lock up my love for Krista and make room in my heart for Julianna.

Don't be afraid to end a relationship with a widower who can't make you number one in his heart and mind. Better to cut your losses than waste your time competing with a ghost, because the ghost will always win.

5. A WIDOWER'S ACTIONS SPEAK LOUDER THAN WORDS

A widower will tell you that he loves you, that

you're pretty, and will say other sweet nothings in order to get attention, sex, companionship, or anything else he wants out of the relationship. A widower's desire to plug the hole in his heart is often so intense that he'll tell you whatever he thinks you want to hear because it feels good to have someone by his side again.

Don't listen to a widower's flattering words. Instead, focus on his actions. If you go to his house and her clothes are still in the closet, her pictures are all over the walls, her ashes are displayed prominently, and her voice is still on the answering machine, it doesn't matter how many times he says he loves you and wants to spend the rest of his life with you. He's not ready to move on and start a new life. If a widower really loves you, his actions and words will align.

When I dated Jennifer, my words and actions never matched up. I told her she was the center of my universe, yet there wasn't one photo of her hanging up at my house. I told her that she was number one in my heart, yet I constantly found myself talking about my late wife, instead of our relationship. I said I wanted to have a future with her, but hesitated in telling my family and friends that I was even dating her.

It wasn't that way with Julianna. I was quick to put photos of her up all over the house. I constantly talked about the life, future, and family I wanted to have with her. I couldn't wait to tell everyone—even complete strangers—that I was dating the most wonderful woman in the world. My actions and words were one and the same. I told her she had the number one spot in my heart, then went out and proved it to her every single day.

STORIES OF WOMEN DATING WIDOWERS

ANN'S STORY

I hesitate to call our courtship and marriage a success because I don't see love and long-term relationships in the black and white manner of women's magazines or dating self-help books. Success is relative even if failure is painted with a universal brush.

When I asked my husband, Rob, why he thought we succeeded when other couples in our situation fail, he replied only half-jokingly, "It was my stellar personality." That's not quite true, but it's not entirely incorrect, either. Relationships that work depend on both partners wanting them to do so.

When we met, I had been widowed for 11 months. Rob's wife had died four months earlier. While I'd begun dating, he'd decided to wait to give himself time to recuperate from Shelley's death and the months he'd spent taking care of her.

We cultivated a "just friends" relationship, which began with meeting via an online widowed support board and eventually took itself offline using email, IM and the telephone.

Rob was the one who suggested elevating our friendship to dating. Before that I was content, despite knowing that our relationship was a bit flirtier than "just friends." However, I didn't try to analyze his actions or read between his words. Like any man, Rob said what he meant, and his actions spoke just as clearly. If a man is interested, he tells you, and if there is a potential long-term option, he acts.

Both of us being widowed probably made things easier. I didn't have to wonder how he felt, nor did I take anything related to his grief personally. Our relationship was a separate issue. Grief is not a *couple's* activity, and it's not an obstacle to moving on with someone else. The right person is more motivation than any widower needs to pack up the past and build a new life. If new love stirred up grief, it was acknowledged, and then we moved on. If he'd hemmed and hawed or had thrown up continual roadblocks in the form of his late wife, children or in-laws, I would have known that he wasn't really serious about us.

How?

I used those things to put off suitors who didn't interest me or with whom I saw no potential for a long-term relationship. It's easier than saying, "I'm not that into you."

Does grief come up? Yes, but only a little bit. If a widower loves you, grief won't derail what you have together. With time, patience and shared effort, you can build a lasting relationship just like any couple does.

Rob made it clear that I was his priority. He was considerate of his daughters' conflicted reactions to us but did not let their grief dictate his decisions. He let family and friends know that he was a grown man who knew his own mind and heart. Not that we met with much active interference or criticism. Most people expressed support and genuine happiness for us.

Bottom line is that our actions set the tone for our children, family and friends. We knew what we wanted, acted accordingly and whatever issues came up were discussed and dealt with immediately—just like any other healthy relationship. Widowed people fall in love, and they do live happily ever after—again.

CHAPTER 2

AVOIDING THE EMOTIONAL ROLLERCOASTER

MOST WOMEN DESCRIBE dating a widower as an emotional rollercoaster ride. All relationships have their ups and downs; however, the peaks and valleys that come with dating a widower tend to happen more often and be higher and lower than in relationships with non-widowed men.

The reason? Many women make excuses for the widower's bad behavior. A common story that finds its way to my inbox goes something like this: A widower will pledge his undying love to the woman he's dating one day, but a day or two later, he'll become withdrawn and tell the woman he's not sure if he's ready for a relationship.

If a single or divorced man behaved in a similar fashion, most women would think the man wasn't ready for a serious relationship and be hesitant to move forward. However, when a man loses his wife, there are women who will wait patiently for months, or even years, for him to get his feelings straightened out. Don't ever do that. Expect the same treatment from widowers as you would single or divorced men. By keeping the same relationship standards, you can avoid or minimize many of the ups and downs that come with dating a widower.

Expect to Be Treated like Number One

Widowers will generally raise or lower themselves to whatever standards they are held to by the women they're dating. If women tolerate feeling like a third wheel in the relationship, most widowers will keep treating them that way, no matter how much it hurts their feelings or drains them emotionally.

Don't be afraid to let him know how you expect to be treated. Women who don't set expectations risk settling for second place over and over again. The best way to let the widower know how you want to be treated is to have open, honest, and loving conversations with him when he does or says something that makes you feel unimportant. Sometimes widowers aren't aware of the emotional pain their behavior and words are causing. A man who loves you and sees a future with you will change his behavior so you feel like a queen. The change may not happen overnight, but you should see him making progress at altering his words and actions.

Soon after Julianna and I started dating exclusively, she took me aside and let me know—lovingly, but in no uncertain terms—that she wasn't going to change the way she wanted to be treated because I had lost a wife. She also told me that she still had reservations about dating a widower, and that if she didn't feel she was number one in my heart, the relationship didn't have a future.

I remember going home feeling hurt and defensive after that talk. I was a little offended that she felt she had to tell me that she expected to be number one. But after sleeping on it and thinking about it during the commute to work the next day, I realized Julianna was right. I had made the choice to start dating again and become exclusive with her. If I was willing to walk that road, I had to make her the most important thing, or the relationship wasn't going to last. Since we had both decided to date only each other, she wasn't asking for anything unreasonable. All she asked was that I walk the walk and not just talk the talk.

Women who don't set expectations with the widowers they're dating risk constantly feeling like he loves his late wife more. You deserve better than that. Don't settle. Let the widower know how you expect to be treated and let him decide whether or not he loves you enough to meet those standards.

ACCEPT THAT THE WIDOWER WILL ALWAYS LOVE THE LATE WIFE

In order for a relationship with a widower to work, you have to be okay with the fact that he will always love his late wife and that she will have a special place in his heart. This doesn't mean you should settle for a relationship where you feel constantly compared to the late wife or like you're competing with a ghost. The human heart has a great capacity for love. You can be loved just as much, or more, than the late wife. However, you have to accept his past and be okay in knowing that the man you love has loved someone else, and still does.

Accepting this isn't always easy. In fact, I can't think of a single woman who's dated a widower who could just accept it without a little hesitation. It was something Julianna struggled with when she was deciding whether we should be exclusive. However, out of the women who have emailed me, those who feel as though they are loved and cherished as much or more than the late wife generally have an easier time dealing with it, while women who feel like a third wheel are the ones who usually struggle.

If a widower's love for the late wife is something you can't live with, end the relationship. Don't tell yourself that you'll get used to it. You won't. There's nothing wrong with opting out. Dating a widower isn't for everyone.

Don't Wait for Him to Stop Grieving

I receive many emails from women who have fallen in love with a widower, only to have the widower tell her that he's still grieving. He won't end the relationship—instead, he asks her to wait, and tells her that he needs some time to sort out his feelings. The question is then asked, how long will it take for him to move on?

Everyone grieves at different speeds. Some people can move on from a tragedy much faster than others. Keep in mind that most widowers generally start dating before they're ready to commit to a long-term relationship. They start the relationship because they're lonely, and then a few months in, they realize they aren't sure if the relationship is right for them. However, they realize that if they end the relationship, they'll be alone again. Instead of manning up, they wuss out and ask the woman to wait. Usually "I'm still grieving" is code for, "I don't love you enough to marry you, but I also don't like the idea of being alone. Please don't leave me!"

In order for a widower to put his feelings for the late wife aside and fully commit to a new partner and new life, he has to have a strong reason to make that change. Most widowers will stop grieving when they find the *right* person—someone that they actually want to start a new life with. I kept the relationship with Jennifer going even when I knew I didn't love her. Had Julianna not come into my life, there's no telling how long I might have kept things going.

Sometimes women have a hard time letting go of the relationship. They believe that if they wait patiently, the widower will move on. But how long are they willing to wait for him to make up his mind? A week? A month? A year?

At the most, I'd give the widower one year of your life—and that's being extremely generous. You should be able to tell within the first few months of dating a widower whether he is ready to stop grieving and if every day you spend with him will be wasted.

Don't be one of the women who waste *years* of their lives. Instead of waiting for him, move on and find someone who will love you for the person you are.

〜

STORIES OF WOMEN DATING WIDOWERS

ANGELA'S STORY

How I knew it was the end: We were together three years and deep down in my heart, I knew he didn't love me the way a man should love a woman. He didn't look at me the way a man who loves a woman with his whole soul looks at a woman. He had a steel wall 10 feet high around him, and I had no hope of ever breaking that down. He would spend hours in a different room from me, and when I would hear that door close, my eyes would well with tears of sadness, rejection and loneliness.

For three years I walked into a home that was supposed to be "ours" and saw nothing but a home filled with W and LW's stuff. "Our" living room was filled with things they bought on their honeymoon; "our" kitchen was filled with their dishes and pottery proclaiming her love for him. "Our" refrigerator was plastered with pictures of them, looking so in love, a look we never had. "Our" hallway had eight pictures of her hanging, and none of us. "Our" house was filled with their life, while my life sat in boxes in the basement. I would bring my stuff up only to hear there was no room and I was too sensitive and needed to get over my issues. I asked him once to take down some of her pictures and make "our" house more about us and less about them. He screamed at me, ripped her pictures up and didn't talk to me for two days. This was two years into the relationship.

I pleaded with him to spend holidays with me instead of her family. He would say he could never imagine hurting them and then he would leave for their house, breaking my heart into pieces as the door slammed shut. Her family would put me down and degrade me, and he would blame it on me. "Well, I guess because of your attitude, I will be going to family functions alone from now on," is what I would hear after complaining because her mom spent the whole night talking about how amazing she was.

I cried night after night alone in the bed we were supposed to share. The couch received all his love at night and kept him warm when it should have been my body. How did I know it was the end? I knew the moment I started dating him. I believed he was damaged and I could fix him, heal him, and that I could be so good to him he would fall in love with me. Instead he left me with nothing but broken promises, a broken heart and the shame of knowing I had just wasted three years of my life with someone incapable of loving anyone but her.

CHAPTER 3:

RED FLAGS TO WATCH FOR WHEN DATING A WIDOWER

MOST WOMEN HAVE dated enough to know which men are worth keeping and which ones to dump. However, because most women have little or no experience with dating widowers, sometimes they don't recognize the red flags that indicate he's not ready for a long-term, committed relationship.

From the emails I've received over the last seven years, my own experience, and conversations with other widowers, I've noticed five reoccurring warning signs that indicate the widower either doesn't love the woman he's dating or isn't ready to let go of the wife he lost.

If a widower has one or two of these red flags, that doesn't mean he can't change, but it should serve as a warning that he may not be ready to make you his top priority.

RED FLAG #1: THE WIDOWER HIDES YOU FROM FAMILY AND FRIENDS

Sometimes it's difficult for a widower to let his friends and family know there's a new woman in his life. Generally, the reason for this is that he is unsure of his feelings for the woman he's dating. Men who really love the women they're with and are ready to move forward will let the world know about the new, special women in their lives.

When I became serious with Jennifer, I didn't let people know I was dating her until a few days before she came to visit me. Looking back, there were several reasons I didn't tell anyone about what I was doing. First, I knew a lot of them were grieving Krista's death and would have a hard time seeing me with someone other than her. Second, I was worried they would think I was moving on too fast, or that they wouldn't be open to the idea of seeing me with someone else.

The biggest reason it took me so long to even tell my family about this woman was that I wasn't completely in love with her. My own doubts about the relationship made it a battle not worth fighting. Why go through the hassle and trouble of having her meet the family when I had my own doubts about the relationship?

When I started dating Julianna seriously, I didn't hesitate to tell everyone I knew about her. I *wanted* them to meet her, to see how wonderful she was and how happy she made me. I didn't care what anyone else thought of her or that we had become serious less than a year after my wife passed away. I knew she was the woman I wanted to marry and wanted everyone else to know that too.

I've received emails from women who have been asked to hide in closets or basements when family unexpectedly dropped by, or who have spent the holidays or other special occasions alone while the widower attended family activities. In each case, the woman has put up with it because they thought the widower or his friends and family needed more time to grieve. I tell these women that unless they like playing the role of a secret mistress, they shouldn't tolerate being hidden from the world. Besides, if the widower can't be honest with his family and friends about his love life, odds are, he's not being honest with you, either.

The only way to fix this problem is for the widower to apologize and immediately introduce his new love to friends and family. Any hesitation on his part means he's harboring doubts about the relationship.

Red Flag #2: You Remind Him of the Late Wife

Widowers are naturally attracted to women who have similar physical and personality traits that remind them of their recently departed wife. They think they can effortlessly form that same deep connection with anyone who looks or acts the same way as their last wife.

When I entered the dating waters again, most of the women I was immediately attracted to had blonde hair and blue eyes, as well as a perky, outgoing personality—all things that reminded me of Krista. Jennifer had many of the same physical and emotional characteristics, and I think that's part of what drew me to her. I quickly learned that despite similar characteristics, Jennifer was very different from Krista, and we didn't have the deeper connection that would lead to a long-term, successful relationship.

When I first met Julianna, there was an immediate physical attraction. But I wasn't attracted to her because she reminded me of Krista. She was simply one of the most gorgeous women I had ever seen. After a couple of dates, I realized we were connecting on a deeper level, and the relationship had the potential to turn into marriage (something we were both seeking) if we could only overcome some of her concerns about dating a widower.

Most women would prefer to be loved for who they are—not who widowers want them to be. If a widower says the woman he's dating acts, thinks, or has other similar qualities to the late wife, the woman should be extremely concerned. The danger here is that the widower is probably using her as a physical and emotional replacement for what he remembers the late wife to be, instead of loving the woman for who she is. Once the widower realizes he's dating a completely different person than the late wife—despite the fact that she looks and acts like the late wife on other levels—the relationship will come to a crashing end.

RED FLAG #3: HIS HOME IS A SHRINE TO THE LATE WIFE

When the late wife dies, she becomes immortalized. It doesn't matter how many faults she had or sins she committed when she was alive; overnight, those things are forgotten, and only her good qualities and characteristics are remembered. The grieving man often plasters photos all over the house or builds shrines to her.

There's nothing wrong with remembering the dead. I had a hallway and bedroom full of pictures of Krista after she died. However, when I become serious with Julianna, I took the photographs and other mementos down as I made room in my heart for new love. Widowers who are ready to start a new life will go out of their way to make their homes comfortable and welcoming to the women they're with. If the widower has minor children living at home, there's nothing wrong with leaving some pictures up for the sake of the children. But it should be done in such a way that the woman should still feel comfortable in the home instead of feeling like the late wife is staring down at her from every wall.

Shrines come in more forms than just photographs

on the wall. Some widowers leave the late wife's clothes and toiletries in her closet or in their bathroom long after she has died, often because it adds a sense of familiarity to the house and keeps it from feeling too empty. But like photos on the wall, the late wife's things are a physical manifestation of where the widower is in terms of grieving and making room for someone else. Widowers who still have their wife's possessions all over the house aren't ready to move on. It doesn't matter how many times he says he loves you—if the late wife's clothes are in the closet, he's not ready to make room in his heart or his home for you.

Red Flag #4: You Constantly Feel Compared to the Late Wife

One of the most difficult things about dating a widower is that the late wife is always viewed as a perfect person—no matter how many mistakes she made while alive. It's hard when friends or family members say something great about the late wife, because whether they mean to or not, they're making an indirect comparison to the new woman in his life.

The truth is every widower will compare the

woman he's currently dating to the late wife. Comparing one person to another is something natural and something we've all done. Widowers are used to a person with specific habits and tastes, and they're going to notice differences. It's just a way for the widower to figure out if he can live with the differences. He'll stop comparing once he's fallen in love again and accepted the new woman in his life for who she is.

The problem comes when a woman feels constantly compared to the late wife by the widower's words or actions. To be fair, not all widowers say things to make the women they're dating feel bad—sometimes they just verbalize what's going through their minds. If it's something he does day after day, it could be an indication he's having a difficult time adjusting to a new relationship. It could also be a sign that he's having a difficult time accepting you for you who are.

The best way to deal with this red flag is to talk to the widower about it. Those who are trying to move on will stop verbalizing their comparisons. As they fall in love with the woman they're with and the relationship grows stronger, they'll appreciate the new woman's unique habits and viewpoints.

RED FLAG #5: HE'S ALWAYS AT THE CEMETERY OR OTHER SPECIAL PLACES

Each widower has his own way of paying his respects to the dead. Some widowers do it by taking trips to places that meant something to the two of them. Others visit the place where her ashes were scattered or the cemetery where she's buried.

While there's nothing wrong with making these visits occasionally, trips to the cemetery tend to pull widowers out of the present and back to the past. Personally, I haven't visited my late wife's grave in seven years. There are a lot of reasons for this, but the biggest is that in order to move forward, I can't live in the past and would rather concentrate on the life and family I have now.

I don't recommend that all widowers stop visiting their late wife's grave. I see nothing wrong with going once or twice a year. However, if widowers insist on visiting more often, I'd be concerned. It could be a sign they're still grieving and aren't ready to progress in a new relationship.

Life is for the living—not the dead. Going to the grave several times a year shows that the heart hasn't healed. There's nothing wrong with remembering the past, but it does no good to live in it.

∾

STORIES OF WOMEN DATING WIDOWERS

ERIN'S STORY

I started dating my widower in October of 2008, not even four months after he lost his late wife due to complications from cystic fibrosis. From the beginning there were the typical issues surrounding dating a widower: pictures of her all over the house, her belongings still in the closets and drawers, drama with his former in-laws being upset that he had started dating so quickly after her death, etc. My initial reaction was to end the relationship before it even began, but I felt a strong connection to him and was hopeful that things would improve as time went on.

Little did I know that one year later, despite our recent engagement and the fact that we were living together, the issues surrounding his being a widower were just as difficult as they were from day one. It didn't matter that her things were removed from the house and that her family was no longer in contact with him. Her presence was everywhere. To make matters worse, we were living in the same house he'd lived in with her, but his job would be transferring soon, so we would be moving to another state. I was hopeful that once we were married and living somewhere else, we could begin our future together, minus the ghost. However, almost every discussion surrounding our wedding and impending move ended with one of us yelling, and the other in tears.

I was terrified that my entire life was going to be spent living in her shadow, feeling like I was never quite good enough. It became obvious to me that my widower had never fully mourned his late wife. I began to notice situations in our day-to-day lives where he found it easier to sweep his feelings under the rug rather than risk upsetting me by speaking up. Also, when talking to outsiders, he'd pretend like that period of his life didn't happen, that he'd been single right up until we met. I wondered if he'd ever find a way to move past his grief and begin his future with me. I suggested he see a therapist, or that we attend couples therapy, but he wanted no part of it.

Unfortunately for me, his grief came to a head five weeks before our wedding and resulted in him calling the entire thing off. I found out weeks later that he was telling people he ended it because I wasn't able to accept the fact that he was married before! In the end, my ex took zero responsibility for his actions and refused to see that his past was standing in the way of his future with me, or anything else. Moving forward was one of the hardest things I've ever had to do, but looking back, he did me the biggest favor of my life by walking away.

I'm now about to marry someone who makes me feel like the center of his world, 24/7. I only hope my ex has gotten the help that he needed, and I truly wish him nothing but the best. My advice to those out there dealing with similar circumstances? Follow your gut. If you feel like you're second, it's probably because you are.

CHAPTER 4:

DATING A WIDOWER WITH CHILDREN

SEEING THEIR FATHER with another woman can be hard on kids, no matter how old they are. Many of them are still grieving their mother's death and can't understand how Dad can move on and "replace" her. It's a natural reaction, and I don't blame anyone for wondering why their father wants to date again. I'd probably have a difficult time seeing my dad with someone else if my mom passed on, if it weren't for my own experience.

My advice on dealing with a widower's children depends on whether the children are minors still living at home, or adults with lives of their own.

As much as you'd expect childish behavior to come

from the children living at home, it usually comes from the adult children who don't live at home. A woman recently emailed me and spoke of how the widower's adult children invited him over for Thanksgiving but made it clear that she was not invited. It was too painful for them to see their dad being affectionate with someone other than their mom. The widower decided to abide by his children's wishes and spend Thanksgiving with them—leaving his new "love" alone on Thanksgiving.

In short, this widower chose his kids, all of whom are grown and have families of their own, over the new woman in his life. Instead of giving in, he should have explained that he was now a package deal and couldn't attend without this special woman.

There's nothing you can do about the thoughts or actions of another person. Don't concern yourself with whether or not his adult children like you or approve of their father dating again. You can always try to win them by showing love and respect, no matter what they say or how they treat you. What you should keep a sharp eye on, however, is how the widower responds to his adult children's juvenile and controlling demands.

You want a widower with a backbone—one who can say *no* to unreasonable demands. If he can't stand up to his children now, odds are he's not going to stand up to them any time Christmas, birthdays, or other special occasions roll around. Instead of being at his side, you're going to find yourself in the number two position time and time again.

Talk about it with him all you want, but odds are that at this stage in the game, if the children are controlling their father, it's not going to change unless the widower puts you first.

When it comes to minor children still living at home, here are some general rules:

- Beware of widowers who are just looking for someone to help out with the kids. I'm amazed at the number of emails I've received from women who have turned into full-time, unpaid nannies with benefits, taking care of the kids by day and having sex with the widower at night. Unless you marry the guy, never forget that his kids are *his* responsibility—not yours. (After you're married, you share the responsibility.)

That doesn't mean you can't help out on occasion, but you shouldn't dedicate your life to raising them unless you become their stepmother.

- Realize that men with minor children might not be able to spend as much "alone time" with you as you both may want. They often find themselves with limited time to be a dad. This means that if he wants to spend time with you, your dates may involve going to his children's soccer games or other activities. One-on-one time is important in any relationship, but it's harder to come by when kids are at home. Understand he has a difficult juggling act but should still be doing his best to show you through his actions that you're number one.

- Don't be jealous of the time and attention he pays to the kids. His minor children living at home should be his top priority. If he's managed to find time for a romantic relationship, that's great, but the wants and needs of his kids should come first. If the relationship is meant to be, both of you will find creative ways to make it work.

- If the kids hate or resent you, treat them with love and respect. You can't control what others think of you. If they say unkind things or try to push your buttons, respond with love and kindness. This is the same advice I give when dealing with others who may not approve of the relationship. It may not be easy to turn the other cheek, but, in the end, you'll win over more people this way.

- Talk to the kids and let them know you're not there to replace their mom. Just because you're part of their life doesn't mean they have to stop loving their mother. Just like it's possible for a widower to make room in his heart for another woman, kids can find a place for more adults. You're an addition, not a replacement.

- If you don't like the way the widower disciplines (or refuses to discipline) his kids, don't expect anything to change once you're in a committed relationship, engaged, or married. Odds are, the discipline (or lack thereof) will continue even after you're the stepmom. If you can't live with it, bail out before it's too late.

<hr/>

STORIES OF WOMEN DATING WIDOWERS

AMY'S STORY

The widower I'm dating has two children, ages three and seven. We have been dating for 11 months, and I see his kids two or three times a week. My relationship with the kids started early on while we were dating. I felt so sad they didn't have a mother, and I would go in their rooms and read to them or just talk.

With the seven-year-old, I would touch base with her every few weeks and ask her how she was doing. She would discuss things with me that she didn't necessarily discuss with her dad. She and I started bonding pretty early on. There were times, on more than one occasion, where I had to excuse myself from the room because my eyes were filled with tears. One of those times, the seven-year-old said she wanted a life-size cutout of her mother so she could hug it all the time. Another time, I was rocking the then two-year-old and singing to him, and the tears started because I was just thinking that his mom should have been the one holding him and loving on him.

The widower and I plan on getting married this year, but we are not in the same house now, so I do not yet have the "mom" role. I do recall a painful comment by the seven-year-old while we were out to dinner. A child thought I was her mom and said a comment to her about it. She said, "Why does everyone think you are my mom? I hate it when people do that." I don't know if this came about because I am, in fact, not her mom, or if she is scared to allow someone else that close to her, in her fear that that another woman has that title besides her real mother. Her dad spoke with her, letting her know it is okay that she has another mom. He explained to his daughter that her mother is never coming back physically. He told her he knows how much she wants her mom back, but no matter what, she won't be back here on Earth.

My hopes are that one day, she and her brother do accept me as their mother. I don't want them to ever forget their mother, and I want them to learn about her. At the same time, I want them to have a living mother that can love them unconditionally, hug them, nurture them, and help raise them.

LESLEIGH'S STORY

I am now engaged to a wonderful widower with whom I'm very much in love. It has been a three-year road of being extremely patient, seeking my own counsel in psychotherapy and continuing to let go of the expectation that my sweetheart's only child, a lovely young 21-year-old woman, would be accepting of me as other than her father's (then) girlfriend and now fiancé.

At the beginning of our relationship, Bryan's daughter, Britney, appeared to be happy that her father was dating, not alone and having some fun again. She was 16 when her mother was diagnosed with cancer and had the horrific responsibility of sometimes even driving her mom to chemotherapy treatments.

When her father and I became closer, it was very

difficult for Britney to accept me in her father's life. I believe that she would have had an easier time perhaps if I hadn't been the first woman that he dated after his late wife passed away. Our relationship was difficult for Britney, and soon I realized that her lack of acceptance had *nothing* to do with me and everything to do with her healing process.

Last year the daughter graduated from college but struggled with inviting me to her graduation because she was so sad that her mom wasn't alive to attend with her father. I didn't go to the graduation. Bryan wanted me by his side, and I wanted to be with him, but it was more important to support his daughter's wishes. This was *her* special event. I had to grow another emotional skin once again.

When Bryan and I became engaged, I received a text from his daughter a few days later saying, "Congratulations!" It didn't make her wrong for not picking up the phone; I just understand that she is doing the best she can to add me into the mix of her life. It has tremendously helped this past year that *she* has an important new man in her own life and doesn't have the need to lean so much on her dad.

I don't expect that Britney and I will be close friends soon. I give her space, and I am respectful. We don't use the word "love," and I accept that she holds me at a distance. It's okay. She is happy that her father is happy now, and we have moved many steps closer in our communication over these three years. My advice to anyone dating a widower with an adult child is to realize that whatever behaviors seem distancing by his adult child/children are not meant personally. Their attitude has a lot to do with simply trying to make sense of their own loss and is trying to move ahead in their own life as best as she/he can.

CHAPTER 5:

HOW TO TALK TO
A WIDOWER

THROUGHOUT THIS BOOK, I've mentioned that the best way to solve an issue with a widower is to talk to him about it. Many times, men are unaware that their habits, behaviors, or words may be causing you to feel like number two. Open communication doesn't come overnight. It's a process of working together and understanding when and how to approach the other person. Never think that a widower doesn't want to talk about relationship issues. If he cares about you and the relationship, he'll talk. The problem is that most women talk about issues with a widower the same way they do with a girlfriend. Widowers are men, and getting them to open up requires knowing how to bring up subjects in a male-friendly way. Here are four tips that can help you talk a widower.

1. NEVER ACT JEALOUS OF THE LATE WIFE

Talking about the late wife, her things, or anything else related to her is like walking through a minefield. Take one wrong step, and the entire relationship will be blown to hell. Remember, widowers will always love their late wife and will take any negative remarks about her personally and will tune out anything else you say.

This doesn't mean the late wife can't be mentioned, or that women have to feel like they're walking on eggshells when the late wife comes up in conversation. What it means is that women have to hide any feelings of jealousy—even if that's the only emotion you have toward her. Attacking the dead or speaking ill of them won't get you anywhere.

2. PICK THE RIGHT TIME TO TALK

Finding the right time to talk to a widower is critical. As you get to know him better, you'll learn the good times to talk about widower-related issues and when to let things slide to another day. If you find the right time, he'll be more receptive to what you want to talk about.

For example, he might really like football. It's Sunday afternoon, and he's kicking back on the couch, watching his favorite team. Trying to talk to him during the game isn't going to get you far. Not only will his attention be divided, but he'll inwardly resent you for bring up the subject during the game. A better alternative is to wait until the game is over. Perhaps suggest that the two of you go for a walk or a drive afterward.

The key to finding the right time is patience. Most issues don't have to be addressed immediately—even if you think otherwise. The widower will be more likely to listen to what you have to say if you can find a time when he'll want to listen and talk to you.

3. SOLVE ONE ISSUE AT A TIME

If there are multiple issues to discuss, pick the most important one and talk about it first. The other issues can wait for another day. Men *hate* being dumped on. They hate feeling like they're not doing things right or that you're complaining about everything. Men are much better at listening and being receptive to what you say when they have to solve one problem a time. Talk about the problem and work on resolving it before bringing up any other issues. Do this, and the widower will be more likely to listen when you need to bring other issues up.

4. KNOW WHAT PROBLEMS YOU NEED TO SOLVE ON YOUR OWN

There are going to be some widower-related issues you need to deal with on your own. This doesn't mean you can't tell the widower about them, but if you do, let him know that he can't help solve them—they're just on your mind.

After Julianna and I became serious enough to discuss the possibility of marriage, she told me there were times when it was hard for her to think about marrying me because a lot of the things that would be firsts for her (marriage, buying a house, and starting a family) were going to be seconds for me. After she told me about this struggle, she said this was something I couldn't solve for her. It was an issue she had to work through on her own, but she wanted me to know how she was dealing with things and would update me occasionally on how she was working through those issues. Not only did this let me know what was going through her mind, but it set an example for me. If she was willing to put the time and effort into working on her problems, I should be willing to work on mine as well.

~~~

STORIES OF WOMEN DATING WIDOWERS

TAMI'S STORY

It was important for me to have an open-door communication policy with my widower. I made it clear from the start that in order for any relationship to work, communication had to be the key. We both made it possible for it to be successful because we both told one another about our desires, what made us happy, what made us mad, what things we looked for in a significant other. My widower had been without his late wife for only six weeks when we started our whirlwind romance. Her death was still fresh, and he was numb. Each day we spent together made it harder for me to understand what he was truly feeling. Most of the time, we were doing normal things you do when you first starting dating someone (movies, dinner, concerts, etc).

After I started to develop stronger feelings, I told him where my heart and mind were. I asked him how he was progressing and if he saw a future for us. At that time, he said he was still in love with her. It was hard being in love with him and to have those feelings not being reciprocated towards me but to a woman who died, wondering if he would ever fall in love with me. He had to reassure me of his thoughts and feelings often. Once I asked him if he had never met her but had met me, if he could see himself falling in love with me. When he answered, "yes," I knew that all I had to do was wait. He had to make the transition of being in love with her for the rest of his life, to loving someone else and possibly falling in love again. He had to be determined to make room for a new love; that's not something I could do for him.

The most important lesson I learned was to be open and patient. I had to be open to the idea that he may or may not fall in love with me, and I had to be patient for him to come to those realizations on his own. He had to make sure whether he was ready or not, there was nothing I could have done to change that. It wasn't about me making him happy, but it was about him finding happiness within himself again. As it turns out, he did fall in love with me, and we are moving forward each and every day. If he had not fallen in love with me, I would have been hurt, but you can't force love on people, widower or not. It has to be mutual.

CHAPTER 6:

Sex and Intimacy with Widowers

Before I dive into this topic, I want to warn you that this chapter isn't for everyone. Each person has their own views about sex and when it's the right time to become intimate with someone you love. I'm not going to tell you when you should or shouldn't sleep with a widower. That's a personal decision you have to make.

The audience for this chapter is women who are thinking about becoming physically intimate with the widowers they're dating, but are worried that he might just be using them for sex instead of taking the relationship to the next level. If this sounds like you, keep reading. If not, I encourage you to at least give this chapter a try. If you're not ready to start thinking about intimacy, skip to the next chapter. You can always come back later when the time is right.

When it comes to sex, most widowers find themselves in a tough spot. When their wife passed on, so did regular sex. The desire for sex is one of the reasons widowers start dating again. As a result, there are a lot of men who will quickly jump into bed with someone, even if they don't have any intention of having a long-term, committed relationship with that person.

My inbox overflows with emails from women who regret sleeping with a widower, only to be dumped the next morning. They feel used and manipulated. If this is something you want to avoid, here are some things you should know that will let you know if the widower is just looking for sexual release or a serious relationship with you.

1. WIDOWERS DON'T EQUATE SEX WITH COMMITMENT

Men and women view sex differently. Most women tend to view sex as a way to get closer to the man they're dating and a way to up the commitment level.

Widowers, on the other hand, generally don't equate sex with commitment—at least, not early on in the relationship.

Even if you give him the greatest sex he's ever had, sex in and of itself won't make the widower want to commit to you. If widowers can get sex from you without giving you their heart, they'll do it. It doesn't matter that he's been married before. Sex won't equal commitment unless he really has feelings in his heart for the woman he's dating.

2. The Widower Won't Mind Waiting

It's okay to say no to physical intimacy right away. A widower who's interested in a long-term, committed relationship will *never* pressure you to sleep with him. He'll patiently wait until you're ready to take this step. Widowers who are just looking for sexual fulfillment will usually complain or threaten to end the relationship if they don't get sex as soon or as often as they want it.

3. The Late Wife Won't Be in His Bedroom

A widower who wants the relationship to be more

than just a good time in bed will make his bedroom a place where you'll feel comfortable. That means he'll remove any photos or personal belongings of the late wife.

A widower who wants to sleep with you while his late wife stares at you from the nightstand or wall probably isn't looking to move on. The same applies if he still has her clothes in the closet and her toiletries in the bathroom. His late wife didn't have to sleep with him while a photograph of his past girlfriend hung on wall. Why should you be treated any differently? If he's ready to love again, making over the room where the two of you spend intimate moments shouldn't be a big deal. It also shouldn't be something you have to ask him to do. It's something he should do on his own.

~

Occasionally I'll get an email from someone who's in a physical relationship with a widower but feels like her performance is being compared to the late wife. This feeling usually doesn't come from something the widower said or did, but the natural insecurities that often come with wondering if you'll ever measure up.

Most widowers don't expect you to be the late wife. Instead of comparing yourself, work on creating a sexual relationship that is unique and fulfilling for the two of you. If you're feeling compared or unfulfilled, talk to the widower about what's working and what's not working in the bedroom. Get the late wife out of your head and concentrate on making the experience something both of you will continue to enjoy throughout your relationship.

STORIES OF WOMEN DATING WIDOWERS

KAREN'S STORY

My fiancé has never made comparisons between his late and me. He appreciates the fact that I am different, and he let me know that from day one. But early on, he wanted to share a couple stories about sex and the late wife. It was his way of showing that he was eager to do whatever he could to please me. Both times, I *shhhhed* him gently.

"What went on in Vegas should stay in Vegas, if you get my drift. I think your late wife would agree."

I don't talk about my bedroom history with anyone, period. Nor do I want to know anyone else's. This has been a personal policy I've always upheld out of respect for myself and for past lovers. Even my future husband doesn't get an exemption. A few times, his curiosity about my sexual past had led me to pull the "Don't ask, 'cause I'm not telling" card on him.

What's important is how you and I enjoy each other now, not what I used to do with someone else.

He nods and thanks me for the reminder.

⌒

MADELYN'S STORY

It was his wife's robe, hanging on a hook in the bathroom, that ended our romance. I hadn't meant to date someone who was involved with another. Call me old fashioned, but I'm not into threesomes, and I have enough self-respect not to cast myself as the "other woman."

My first date with Will was great. We went to dinner and didn't stop talking for a good three hours. During that date Will told me about his late wife, Christine, how they had been married for 40 years, and that she had died of cancer two and a half years ago. However, when Will talked about his home he referred to it as "their" house and where "they" lived. A little confused, I tried to clarify if there was someone he lived with, but he insisted there wasn't anyone else. When I finally went to his house, the living room was one that had been preserved, almost eerily so, since the day Christine had died. There were easily 20 pictures of the woman spanning their entire married life displayed on every piece of furniture, wall, nook and cranny.

Our relationship progressed, and over the next few months, Will and I saw each other several times per week. I enjoyed his company, craved our incredible sexual encounters, but felt that there was a part of him that was absent—present but not accounted for. I also questioned his allegiance. His constant use of plural pronouns and references to Christine made me think that he'd give anything to have her back in his life. Given that he couldn't make that happen, I wondered if I was a mere consolation prize. Wasn't I worth more?

It was a Sunday morning after we had made love. Will always wore a gold necklace with a medal on it, and I had never really looked at it closely before. I asked him about it now, and he told me that it was a medal of St. Christopher then explained that his wife had wanted a St. Christopher's medal after completing her first bout of chemotherapy. They had searched and searched for just the right medal until they found this one. St. Christopher is the patron saint of travelers, and Christine wanted to be protected by her namesake for whatever lay ahead.

It was a very touching story, but the weird vibes descended upon me again, this time in a heavy shroud. Was Christine somehow with us every time we had sex? Was she somehow hypnotizing me when Will and I were doing it?

I went to the bathroom. I looked up at the two bathrobes hooked to the back of the door, and I couldn't help but ask Will if one of the robes was Christine's. He said it was. She had been dead two and a half years and still had a hook in the bathroom for her robe?

And then it hit me. I was with someone else's lover, not mine. I couldn't get out of "their" house fast enough. I phoned Will later and told him I felt like I was part of a threesome, and it didn't feel good. I men-

tioned his pronoun usage, the photos, and the necklace. He said he was sorry I felt that way, but he really
liked his life the way it was. He thought the best thing
for us to do was not to see each other.

And just like that, it was over.

CHAPTER 7:

FAMILY AND FRIENDS
WHO CAN'T MOVE ON

ONE OF THE MOST nerve-wracking aspects of any relationship can be meeting his parents, extended family, and close friends for the first time. When dating a widower, meeting those he loves can be even more stressful, because the widower is usually starting a new life with someone before family and friends have finished grieving. This means that in addition to the stress of hoping everyone approves, there's the additional anxiety that comes from wondering if they're going to accept you for who you are, or let you know how much better the late wife was.

The good news is that most people, even if they're

still mourning, will be happy the widower has found a new love and will do their best to welcome you into their circle of family and friends. However, there seems to be always one person who has a hard time seeing the widower with someone other than his late wife. (For issues about the widower's adult and minor children, refer to Chapter 4. This chapter specifically deals with his extended family, the late wife's extended family, and close friends he and the late wife had.)

Just a few of the horror stories that have been emailed to me over the years include family and friends always talking about the late wife when the new woman's around, being purposely not invited to family get-togethers and parties, and being flat out ignored by the widower's close circle of friends. In short, instead of being made to feel like part of the family, the new woman is treated like an outsider or a mistress. She's made to feel that she's not wanted and will never be as good to the widower as the late wife.

Julianna and I were fortunate in that pretty much all my family and friends were polite and accepting of her and our relationship. Even though I knew many family members and close friends were struggling with my decision to date and remarry so soon after Krista's death, they did their best to welcome Julianna into the family and accept her for who she was.

Still, there were moments when people said or did something that made it tough for Julianna to feel like she was welcome. For example, when we announced our engagement to my family, my mom told everyone that she recently had a dream about Krista, and that wherever she was, Krista was happy so it was okay if we got married. Her comments sucked the excitement from the room and made most of those who were there uncomfortable.

I don't think my mom was trying to be hurtful to me and Julianna, or even trying to detract from our special moment. Looking back, I believe she was trying to let everyone else know that she thought it was okay that I was moving on and remarrying. Still, she could have picked a better way and a more opportune time to express these feelings.

Whatever people do or say—intentional or otherwise—it's important not to take their comments or actions personally. In most cases, those who behave this way are still grieving the loss of their daughter, sister, mother, or friend. For whatever reason, they're having a hard time moving on and are having difficulty accepting the fact that the widower has fallen in love with someone else. Sadly, many of them are going to take it out on you.

No matter how poorly you're treated, it's important that you react to these situations with love and kindness. Just like a widower's actions speak volumes about how he really feels about you, how you respond to these situations will show the late wife's family what kind of person you are. If you respond to their impolite comments with love, you'll end up with friends instead of enemies. Odds are, most of those who are having a hard time now will eventually come around to accepting you and the new relationship. It's a lot easier for them to do that when you've been kind in return.

Under no circumstances, however, should you nurture unhealthy relationships or keep putting yourself in places where you have to deal with people who want to make your life a living hell. For example, if the widower likes to get together for a monthly gathering with family members who don't make you feel welcome, don't go. Explain the situation to the widower and how uncomfortable some people at the event make you feel. Start this dialogue, because the widower needs to know exactly what's going on. If things don't improve, the widower's probably going to choose between you and the person who can't let go of the past. And widowers who are ready to move forward won't have a problem choosing you.

Once a widower knows about a situation, he needs to politely tell others that you are part of his life and they need to extend the same love and kindness to you as was extended to the late wife. There are many ways to do this without hurting anyone's feelings. When the widower doesn't stand up for you, what he's really saying is he values the feelings and relationships of his friends and family more than he values yours. In short, he's treating you like second best.

A widower who really loves you will defend you and let the offending parties know in a kind, loving way that their behavior is off-base. Widowers who let their family and friends treat you like a second-class person are not worthy of your love. After all, if he didn't let others treat the late wife this way, why should you expect this kind of treatment?

THE LATE WIFE'S FAMILY

Sometimes the widower is very close with his late wife's family. This means that aside from introducing you to them, he may want to continually spend time with them. Even if the former in-laws are polite and accept their former son-in-law's decision to date and marry again, spending lots of time with them can be difficult for women dating widowers.

From the emails I've received, most women don't seem to mind if the widower they're dating has a relationship with the in-laws. Many even get along with the late wife's family just fine. The problem usually arises when the widower has such a strong relationship with them that the woman feels like the amount of time they're spending with the former in-laws is coming between her and the widower.

If you feel the widower's spending too much time with the late wife's family, talk to him about it. Sometimes spending lots of time with the former in-laws may just be part of his life—especially if he and the late wife had children. Sometimes the late wife's family steps in to help, and he's used to having them around. If he's unaware how the time spent with them is affecting you, simply letting him know your thoughts and feelings about the situation can go a long way to solving the problem.

Spending too much time with the in-laws isn't something Julianna and I had to deal with. I wasn't on good terms with Krista's parents when she died. Krista's brother and grandmother were the only people I had a relationship with. Though we did spend some time together, it was never enough for Julianna to feel like any time spent with them was interfering with my relationship with her.

So how much should the late wife's family be part of your life? Well, it depends. If the widower and the late wife had children together, odds are the late wife's family is going to be more of a presence than if they had no children. In the end, it's going to have to be something that both you and the widower can live with. Just keep in mind that if he's on good terms with the former in-laws, you need to decide if having them being part of your life is something you can live with. If you can't live with it, and the widower is unwilling to budge, then it might be time for you to move on.

STORIES OF WOMEN DATING WIDOWERS

RACHEL'S STORY

When John and I began dating, he told me how much he loved and adored his folks—and how much they would love me. While they lived hundreds of miles away, they were a tight-knit family, even more so following Kristen's death two years earlier. So I was excited to meet them.

When I arrived at John's house—the same house he shared with Kristen—his parents greeted me with smiles and open arms. His stepmom, Carol, asked about my favorite movie, my favorite books, my hobbies.

"Those were Kristen's favorites, too," she said.

I felt my face flush at the mention of Kristen's name, but I also felt a strange kinship to the woman who came before me.

Maybe our similarities bode well for my relationship with Carol, I thought.

I soon realized that Carol was still reliving every

memory, every moment, every facet of Kristen's life, even celebrating John and Kristen's anniversary with dinner at their reception site, followed by a viewing of their wedding video late into the night. Even worse, Carol always addressed Kristen as "you know who" when I was in the room. I felt like she was pitting me against Kristen, expecting that the mere mention of her name would make me feel weak and insecure. And it did, but only because Carol ensured that every conversation evolved into a tribute to Kristen. When I changed the subject, Carol lost interest. But instead of bowing out of the conversation, I found myself comforting Carol, indulging her stories and asking questions about Kristen. I learned that was the *only* way I could connect with Carol. At the time, it didn't occur to me that her behavior was inappropriate, or that playing the role of psychologist for my future mother-in-law wasn't healthy for either one of us.

This twisted relationship turned toxic almost immediately after John and I got engaged. When I called Carol to share my joy and excitement, 95 percent of our conversation was about Kristen and her marriage to John. Instead of setting boundaries and shifting the conversation onto more neutral ground, I fed into Carol's grief, promising to honor Kristen's memory.

"It's great that you're not intimidated by a ghost," she said, while at the same time placing Kristen on an unattainable pedestal.

Things continued to get worse. Thankfully, John stood up for me. He told his parents that unless they could respect the two of us and the lives we were building together, they weren't welcome in our home or in our lives.

I never became a saint like Kristen, but I did gain wings. I learned to stand up for myself, establish boundaries and no longer cater to Carol's needs at the expense of my own. My in-laws' home will continue to be adorned with pictures of Kristen and John on their wedding day, with nary a photo of John and me in sight. They'll continue to talk to John only on holidays. When *he* calls. And even though John and I have been married for two years, they will do their best to pretend I don't exist. And you know what? I'm okay with that.

While I don't have the fantasy in-laws I pictured when John raved about his folks during our courtship, my marriage is better than I ever imagined—in part because we learned to cope with adversity before we even said "I do." Carol has chosen to live in the past where her relationship with Kristen is completely intact. John and I are stepping into the future, celebrating every day we have together and hoping maybe one day, she'll join us.

CHAPTER 8:

HOLIDAYS AND OTHER SPECIAL OCCASIONS

HOLIDAYS, BIRTHDAYS, ANNIVERSARIES, and other specials occasions are generally times most people look forward to and enjoy. For women dating widowers, these special days can be stressful because some men have a hard time letting go of the past, or the late wife is often remembered at these events.

During the last holiday season, several women sent me worried emails about celebrating the holidays with the widower they were dating. One lady wrote to me concerned that the Thanksgiving dinner she was attending would include a toast to the late wife. Another woman was worried about her widower wanting to scatter the late wife's ashes on a ski slope on Christmas Eve. A third was worried about a widower who insists on visiting the cemetery Christmas morning and how that might affect his attitude for the rest of the day. You get the picture.

Holidays can be tough on anyone who's lost a loved one. Generally, the first holiday season without the late wife is the hardest, because the widower's learning how to adjust to life without his wife. Once a widower has made it through their first holiday without the late wife, subsequent holidays are generally easier.

My suggestion on how to handle these situations depends on 1) how long ago the late wife died and 2) how the widower acts during these events. For example, I didn't see a problem with the first widower's Thanksgiving toast, because this was the family's first holiday season without the late wife. Instead of focusing on the toast, I suggested the woman watch how the widower treated her during the time before and after that moment. Did he seem focused on the late wife and the past, or her and the present? Was he introducing her to friends and family, or letting her fend for herself? Was he doing his best to make the day festive, or did it feel like a wake? So long as the widower was doing his best to make the day special for her and treating her like number one, I didn't see a problem with the toast.

I was a little more concerned with the widower who wanted to scatter the ashes on Christmas Eve. First, he brought up the scattering the ashes *after* the two of them had already booked their trip. Second, the wife had been dead two years, and I found it odd that he was choosing their trip for such a sentimental act. Sure, it might have been his way to saying good-bye and move on, but doing it during a trip that was supposed to create new holiday memories with another woman seemed like awfully bad timing. My suggestion was to talk to him and see what the reason was for doing it during their trip and ask if there was a better time to do it that wouldn't distract from the fun trip they were to enjoy together.

I was extremely worried about the widower who wanted to visit the cemetery on Christmas morning. The day held no significance in his relationship to the late wife aside from the normal holiday stuff. They weren't married on that day, she didn't die on that day, nor did any special event in their marriage happen on that day. It's just something he had done every Christmas (and on every other major holiday) since his wife died five years ago. The woman said that after he visits the cemetery, he comes home quiet and moody—not exactly the best way to usher in the spirit of Christmas. Where the wife's been dead five years, and he won't go to the cemetery the day before or after Christmas, it appears like he's still grieving and not ready to move on. I suggested that unless the widower was willing to forgo or delay the cemetery visit, it would probably be best if she spent the holidays elsewhere. In the meantime she might want to think about whether the widower is ready to start a new life with her.

Be concerned if the widower refuses to make some new traditions that the two of you can call your own. One woman wrote and told me how the widower wanted to take her on a Christmas trip to California because that's where he and the late wife always spent the holiday. While she wasn't opposed to going out of town, she suggested that they go somewhere else just as sunny and warm as California. He refused and said that it wouldn't be Christmas unless they spent that week in San Diego. To me that's a sign that he's living in the past.

First, talk to the widower and see why he feels strongly about upholding certain traditions. Hopefully, he'll be willing to add some of yours to the list or create new ones the two of you can call your own. If he refuses to budge, it could indicate reluctance to move on. Whatever the reason for his refusal to compromise, it doesn't bode well for your relationship. You're a new person. If the widower's willing to start a new relationship, he should be willing to start new traditions, too. You may want to consider spending the holidays with friends and family who can make this time of year more enjoyable.

If there are minor children living at home, I'm more tolerant of keeping some traditions around, especially if their mother is recently deceased. This can give children a sort of normalcy to hold on to during holidays and other special occasions. But it's important that the two of you start making your own traditions. Just because there are minor children doesn't excuse the widower from trying something new.

I know from my own personal experience that holidays and other special occasions can feel empty without the deceased wife by your side. I couldn't wait for my first Christmas without her to be over, because all I could think about was that she wasn't around. However, widowers who have chosen to become part of a committed relationship need to man up and make the holiday season enjoyable for the new woman in their life. That might mean trying out a new tradition, spending a day with her friends and family or just enjoying some alone time with the new woman. It doesn't mean sitting at home sulking or becoming withdrawn and uncommunicative or pretending that the world will go on as it has before. While there's nothing wrong with remembering the past, living in the present, counting our blessings, and creating new memories with a new love are much happier and productive ways to spend the holidays.

Stories of Women Dating Widowers
TAMI'S STORY

When a special "Late Wife" day comes along I make sure to ask him how his day is. In the first year after she died, special days were still fresh and painful. He did a lot of thinking and remembering. I made it known to him that I would be there for him, and also tried to lift his spirits. Yes, he was sad. He's probably going to be sad for a long time, but I'm here. I can hug him, kiss him, and show him that he's not alone.

I was scared, in the beginning, that I would crowd him on these days, craving too much attention towards me, but he did that on his own. On special days like her birthday, their anniversary or the day he proposed to her, he said that he reflected and remembered her on that day, but for the most part it was just another regular day for him. It does not take away from what we have. I have special days with loved ones too, and can look back and remember good times with them, but my life is still going on and so is his. He acknowledges this simple fact—life does go on—and he is doing just that.

CHAPTER 9:

NEVER SETTLE

OCCASIONALLY I'LL RECEIVE an email from someone who's dating a widower who is doing a decent job of moving on and treating the new woman like number one. However, there are other issues in the relationship that the woman is having a hard time with. For example, the widower may be a complete slob and the woman a neat freak, and his messy house is driving her crazy.

Other times the widower may be addicted to alcohol, drugs, or pornography. Sometimes the widower has lots of consumer debt, has difficulty getting it on in the bedroom, or can't find steady employment. Other times it may boil down to different religious or political views coming between the couple. Whatever the problem is, the question I'm usually asked is whether or not it's worth waiting around to see if things improve.

My advice is always the same: Never settle for a relationship with *anyone* if the person has any issue or habit you can't live with. Dating a widower is more than just making sure he's moved on and is ready to start a new life. It's about knowing he is someone you can see yourself spending the rest of your life with *if he never changes*.

For example, my late wife and I were both pretty good when it came to living within our means. We never spent more than we earned and were always trying to put some money away for a rainy day. It was nice not to have money issues and the stress that accompanied it hanging over our marriage.

When I started dating again, I quickly realized that the new women didn't have the same discipline when it came to money-related issues as my late wife. As I dated around I came to the conclusion that I'd have a hard time spending my life with someone who could spend more money than we earned and had mountains of unpaid consumer debt. It didn't matter how beautiful or smart the woman was; it was simply something I couldn't live with. While dating Julianna, it was a relief to know she had the same view about finances, money, and spending as I did. If anything, the fact that she had good money-management habits made her *more* attractive to me.

On the other hand, there were issues I didn't worry about. For example, I couldn't have cared less whether she liked country or rap music, whether she was a morning or a night person, or loved or hated sushi. Those things weren't deal breakers. When I married her, I assumed that there was a zero chance she may never like sushi. Eight years in, she still hates it. However, I knew I could live with her and love her even if she never ate a bite for the rest of our lives together. On the other hand, I knew I was marrying someone who had similar values and beliefs as mine. On the issues I was unwilling to compromise on, Julianna fit the bill. I never settled when I married her. I got someone who was the perfect companion for me and someone I knew I could love no matter what life threw at us.

Life is short. We can choose to live it with someone who we can love or someone who will drive us crazy with worry because they have issues we can't live with. Others may like relationship drama, but I prefer waking up next to someone I can't wait to spend another day with. Whoever you become involved with in a relationship, at some point you're going to know whether or not he is someone you can see yourself spending the rest of your life with. It is at that moment we need to have the courage to either live with it or move on. It may not be an easy choice, but it's one that can have a profound effect on the rest of your life. Therefore, choose wisely.

~

STORIES OF WOMEN DATING WIDOWERS

DEANNE'S STORY

If you are dating a widower who cannot put his past relationships into his past, then he is not ready to move forward. Being a widower does not give anyone the right to treat his current significant other as second best under any circumstances.

As a woman who dated and later married a widower, I expected to be treated as the most important woman in his life, just as I treated him as the most important man in my life. Does he think about his late wife periodically? I'm sure he does. Do I think about my ex-husband periodically? Absolutely. However, we both recognize that those relationships are *in* the past!

I cleared up any ambiguity with my husband early on in our relationship when we were spending one of our first holidays together. My husband (we were not married at the time) mentioned that he would be inviting his former in-laws (late wife's family) over for the holiday because that had been their tradition. I responded that I would also be inviting my former in-laws over for the holiday as well. He was quite surprised by my response, and he was not amused, but I got my point across very clearly. We decided that it was time for both of us to start new traditions! Since that time, I have always been consulted on who we would be sharing our time with.

CAROLYN'S STORY

After ten years of being a divorcée and working my way unsuccessfully through match.com and other dating websites, I decided to give up looking and just have fun. That was when my next-door neighbor asked me to let his father run around with me to dance classes, plays, and bluegrass concerts.

The first time we had dinner, he informed me that we were not "dating." I responded of course not, we are just hanging out together. After seven occasions of "hanging out," he kissed me. I advised him that I didn't kiss my hanging-out friends in that manner. He said that he had changed his mind and wanted to date me. After four months of dating, he told me that he hoped that I was not expecting marriage, as he had no intentions of ever marrying again. I told him that I was living in the present and not the future—therefore I was taking it one day at a time and had no expectations. Once upon a time, I wanted to remarry and was actively seeking a spouse. I now know that until my W gets further along in his grieving process, he is not marriageable material.

Since I was the first woman he seriously dated after the death of his wife, I suggested that he might want to date other women. He didn't like that idea and asked me to just be patient with him.

I have discovered that dating a widower is very different than dating a divorced man. Choices have to be made regarding what you will tolerate (jewelry, constant talk about his wife, comparisons, and lots of mementoes of his late wife) and how long you will tolerate them. Divorced men don't have as much of a problem telling you that they love you, as they don't feel as if they were being disloyal to anyone.

Some days it was very hard when he told my friends and family about things he and his late wife did together. They looked embarrassed for me. I finally realized that his nearly five decades with his LW was the only point of reference he had when meeting new people. He and I have been slowly building experiences together, and the referral back to his LW has slowed down considerably.

Would I date a widower again? Absolutely. My widower has all the qualities of a significant other that I have always wanted. He is well worth being around and having patience that things will change. The bottom line when dating a widower is that you must have patience for him to work through his grieving process. Things do change, although it will not be as quick as most women would want.

CHAPTER 10:

TEN DATING TIPS FOR WIDOWERS

I'M INCLUDING THIS SECTION of the book specifically for any widowers who might be reading it. Dating again after the death of a spouse can be an awkward experience. It can bring out feelings of guilt or betrayal in the widow or widower. It can also bring out feelings of confusion and concern from friends, family, and those who were close to the deceased spouse.

For those who have lost a spouse and are looking to date again, here are ten tips to help you successfully navigate the dating waters.

1. **When you decide to date again is up to you**

There's no specific time period one should wait before dating again. Grieving and the process of moving on is something that's unique to each person. Some people take years, others weeks, and then there are those who choose never to date again. Whatever you do, don't let others tell you you're moving too fast or waiting too long. Make sure it's something you're really ready to try before taking that step.

I started dating five months after my late wife died. Too soon? There were some friends and family who thought so. But five months was when I felt ready to at least test the dating waters. And though it took a few dates to get the hang of things, I have no regrets about dating that soon.

2. **Make sure you're dating for the right reasons**

If you feel like dating again, take some time to understand why you have this desire. It's not wrong to date because you're lonely or want company. Single people date for those reasons too. However, if you're dating because you think it's going to somehow fill the void or heal the pain that comes from losing a spouse, it's not going to happen. Dating does give you the opportunity to open your heart to another person and the chance to experience the unique and exquisite joy that comes with falling in love again.

3. FEELING GUILTY IS NATURAL—AT FIRST

The first time I went to dinner with another woman, I felt like I was cheating on my late wife. As we entered the restaurant, I was filled with feelings of guilt and betrayal. Throughout our entire date, I kept looking around to see if there was anyone I knew in the restaurant. I thought that if someone saw me out with another woman, the first thing they'd do was run and tell my dead wife what I was up to. It sounds silly, but I couldn't shake that feeling the entire evening. A week later, I went out with someone else. The same feelings of guilt were there, only they were less intense. It took about five dates before the feeling went away entirely and I could actually enjoy the company of a woman without feeling guilty.

As you date, feelings of guilt should subside over time—especially when you find that special someone. If the guilt's not subsiding, you might not be ready to date again. Give dating a break and try it again when you might be more up to the task.

4. It's Okay to Talk About the Deceased Spouse—Just Don't Overdo It

Unless you're dating someone you knew previously, and they are already familiar with your late spouse, he or she is naturally going to be curious about your previous marriage. It's okay to talk about the spouse when you're first dating someone. Answer questions he or she may have about your marriage, but don't spend all your time talking about the dead or how happy you were. After all, your date is the one who's here now. And who knows—she might make you incredibly happy for years to come. Constantly talking about the past may make it seem like you're not ready to move on and start a new relationship. Showing a genuine interest in your date and getting to know *her* wants, interests, and dreams goes a long way you're ready to start a new life with someone else.

5. YOUR DATE IS NOT A THERAPIST

Would you like going out with someone who constantly talks about issues she's having in her life? Dating isn't a therapy session—it's an opportunity to spend time with someone else and enjoy their company. If you find yourself dating just to talk about the pain in your heart, how much you miss your spouse, or tough times you're going though, seek professional help. Spending $60 an hour on professional help will do you much more good than spending the same amount of money for dinner and a movie. Besides, your date will have a more memorable night if it's about him or her rather than about everything you're going through.

6. IT'S OKAY TO MAKE MISTAKES WHEN YOU'RE FINDING YOUR DATING LEGS

When I started dating again, it had been seven years since I had gone out with anyone other than my wife. Because I had a certain comfort level with her, I often found myself forgetting proper dating etiquette, such as opening the car door or walking a date to her door when the date was over.

If you find yourself forgetting simple dating etiquette, don't worry about it. Most dates will understand if they know it has been awhile since you dated. But don't make the same mistakes over and over. Learn from them and continue moving forward. You'll be surprised how fast your dating legs return.

7. DEFEND YOUR DATE

When your family and friends learn you're dating again, they may not treat this new person in your life very well. The mistreatment may come in the form of a cold shoulder at family activities or constantly talking about the deceased wife in front of the date. If you have family and friends who are doing this, they need to be told privately, but in a loving manner, that this behavior is not acceptable. If you wouldn't let family or friends treat your spouse that way, why would you tolerate that behavior toward someone else—especially when your date could become your future spouse? Don't be afraid to defend your date. If you can't do that, then you have no business dating again.

8. REALIZE THAT NOT EVERYONE WILL UNDERSTAND WHY YOU'RE DATING AGAIN

There will always be someone who will not understand why you've chosen to date again. They may give you a hard time or have some silly notion that widows and widowers shouldn't fall in love again. Their opinions do not matter. All that matters is that you're ready to date again. You don't need to justify your actions to them or anyone else.

9. TAKE THINGS SLOW

The death of a spouse means losing intimate physical contact. After a while, we miss the kisses, having someone's head resting on our shoulder, or the warm body next to us in bed. This lack of physical and emotional intimacy is enough to drive a lot of people into the dating scene. Don't feel bad if you find yourself missing these things. It's completely normal.

In the dating world, wanting something that was part of our lives for years can become a ticking time bomb. It can force us into a serious relationship before we're ready. The result: a lot of broken hearts and emotional baggage.

If you're on a date and it's going well, don't be afraid to take things slow. This isn't always easy. Sometimes it's hard not to throw ourselves at our date because we want to be close to someone again. We want that warm body next to ours and to have the words "I love you" whispered in our ears. But it can save you and your date a lot of emotional heartache if you wait to make sure what you're doing is because you love the other person, and not because you miss the intimacy that came with your late husband or wife.

10. MAKE YOUR DATE FEEL LIKE THE CENTER OF THE UNIVERSE

It's a basic dating rule, but it's often forgotten by widows and widowers. Because we already had someone special in our lives, it's easy to forget to make our date feel special too. Treat your date in such a way that he or she feels like she's with a man who's ready to move on. She shouldn't have to compete against a ghost— even if you only have one date with that person. As long you're out together, she should feel special.

Even though dating can be awkward and difficult at times, it can also be a lot of fun. There's no reason being a widower should hold you back from enjoying a night out. Part of the reason we're here is to live and enjoy life. And dating is a great way to start living again.

∼

PEGGY'S STORY

The man I am dating is a widower and someone I knew while his wife was alive. I liked them both and thought they were a great couple. I had been divorced by the time we all met.

A few months ago, his wife was killed in a tragic accident. I thought about him and wondered how he and his children were getting along. Suddenly he was thrown into the role of caretaker of children, house, animals, carpools, appointments, dance practice, kid scheduling and management, in addition to the already full-time position of sole financial provider. I was exhausted thinking about it.

Then he called me. We shared a glass of wine and became good friends. He has handled the transition into his new life with realistic expectations. He has been forthcoming about his wife, his children, his relationship with me, and what the community thinks about us as a couple. I am not offended when he tells stories about his wife. That would be absurd on my part. She was his main companion for more than 20 years. No one expects him to erase her from his memory.

He has not made her into a saint. She was a real person with real qualities and imperfections. I am different enough from her that he has not compared us in any way. I don't feel like I'm expected to replace her. He doesn't need someone to do household chores.

A man needs someone to talk to and laugh with, someone who cares about him and is relieved when they receive a text saying his flight landed safely. Everyone wants to know that someone cares about them.

His teenage children live at home with him. He has had frank conversations about going on without their mother. He assured them that while he will never stop loving her, it would be unrealistic to think he would live his life alone and sad.

The kids know me as a mom from school, but they had a mother and she did a great job raising them with her limited time. They are well-rounded kids and will do well, in part due to her influence on them, but also because of the way their dad has modeled how to handle grief and loss. He has shown them that life is for the living, and they should continue to do just that.

The *right* amount of time to grieve is different for everyone, and at some point, a person just needs to be allowed to be happy again. I have learned a lot about grief after tragedy from him.

I doubt very much that either of us would have chosen the paths our lives have taken, but the end result seems to have brought us together. This has been very good for me, and it seems to be good for him, too.

Experience is not what happens to a man. It's what a man does with what happens to him. Becoming a widower is something that happened to him. But he has not let it define him as a man.

CHAPTER 11:

MARRIED TO A WIDOWER

WHEN I ASKED Julianna to marry me, I knew I was doing the right thing. Even though it was just 13 months since Krista had died, I knew I had found someone with whom I could spend the rest of my life.

Still, when I got down on my knee and asked Julianna to be my wife, there was a small part of me that wondered if she'd say "Yes." I knew she loved me, and over the last couple months had talked at length about getting married, but there was a crumb of doubt that made me wonder that, when push came to shove, if she'd be willing to start a life with me at her side.

I knew that the thought of spending her life with a widower was something Julianna had struggled with. She had told me once that *if* we ever got married, she didn't want to play second fiddle to Krista. She would only marry me if she was certain I was ready to start a new life with her. Over the seven months we dated, I had done everything I could in my actions and words to let her know she occupied the top place in my heart. Would it be enough?

So when I got down on the snow-covered ground and popped the question, the biggest smile I'd ever seen burst across her face. I knew what her answer would be before she said anything.

"Yes! Yes! Of course I will!" she said and threw her arms around me.

Two months later we were married.

It's been eight years since we exchanged vows. Since then we've bought a house and started a family, and experienced times of plenty and other days where we barely had enough to make ends meet. For us life has been one unpredictable adventure, but we've made each other and our happiness our top priority. Because of that, our relationship and marriage is stronger than it ever has been. I've never been so in love with someone, and I can't imagine life without Julianna playing a big part of it. Starting over forced me to realize how short and precious life is. Those we love can pass on to the next life at any time. That's why I choose to make Julianna number one in my life each day.

Some people say that marriage to a widower is a relationship of three hearts, with the new woman and the late wife each getting an equal share. I disagree. A successful marriage to a widower requires it to be two hearts—yours and his. The widower will always love his late wife, but in order for a marriage to work, it has to be your heart and his beating in unison. Feelings for the late wife have to be put in a special place, or else you're always going to feel like you're competing with a ghost. And if you feel that way, there's no way the relationship is ever going to last.

If you're going to marry a widower, you need to feel like the only woman he's ever loved. Don't ever deceive yourself into thinking things will improve *after* you get married, because they won't. Widowers treat the women they love like a queen. No exceptions. If a widower asks you to marry him, there should be no doubt that it's the right thing to do. If you have doubt or worry something's wrong—it probably is.

I know Julianna feels like the number one person

in my life. But don't take my word for it. It's best if Julianna explains in her own words how she feels about being married to me.

⇌

JULIANNA'S STORY

I still remember the moment when Abel dropped the widower bomb on me. We were in the middle of dinner on our first date. After I learned he was a widower, I wanted to run from the restaurant where we were eating and never see him again. Dating a widower was something I had never considered. I was 23 at the time and really didn't want to date someone who had been previously married, let alone someone whose wife had died six months earlier.

The rest of the evening went downhill from there. Thankfully it didn't last much longer. After Abel dropped me off at my apartment, I drove to my parents' house and told them about the horrible date. When I told them I never wanted to see Abel again, my dad said Abel deserved a second chance.

I was stunned. A second chance? Was he serious?

Did he really want me dating someone who had just lost his wife? Didn't he think there was someone better out there for me?

So when Abel asked me out a second time, I said "Yes" but told myself this was the last date the two of us would ever go on. But there was a third date, a fourth, then a fifth. Each date got a little bit better and soon we were spending practically every day with each other. It wasn't long before I realized I was in love with Abel. But could I spend the rest of my life with a recent widower?

I realized I had to make a decision soon. It wasn't fair to either of us to continue a relationship if I couldn't accept Abel's past. I knew I had to move forward with Abel, or I had to end things. I thought long and hard about the decision. In the end I chose to commit my heart to Abel. My love for him was only part of the decision. Abel worked hard to make me the center of his universe. He wasn't perfect at it, but I felt that our relationship was always moving forward in the direction of marriage—something we both wanted. On the day he surprised me with a wedding proposal, I couldn't help but say "Yes!" I knew he was the man I wanted to spend the rest of my life with.

Our eight years together haven't been perfect. Like all couples, we've had our good days and our bad ones. But even during the hard times, I've always known that Abel loves and accepts me for who I am and that I occupy the top place in his heart. I don't worry about competing with a ghost because that rivalry isn't there. Our marriage is the two of us moving forward together and putting each other first.

Marrying a widower wasn't something I ever thought about until I met Abel. But looking back, I realize that dating a widower was a blessing in disguise. It forced us both to decide what we wanted from the relationship and, once we were both committed, to make the necessary sacrifices to make the other person number one. Because of this our relationship is rock solid, and I'm looking forward to a lifetime together.

ACKNOWLEDGMENTS

THIS BOOK wouldn't have been possible without all those women who were brave enough to share their stories with the world. I thank you all from the bottom of my heart for letting others read and benefit from your stories.

In addition I'd like to thank Fran Platt for her awesome cover design and typesetting, Tristi Pinkston and Lu Ann Staheli for their editing and suggestions, and Annette Lyon and Trina Livingston for proofreading the manuscript.

Most of all, I'd like to thank Julianna for giving me the time to write another book about widowers and share moments from our personal life with the world. None of my books are possible without your love and support.

ABOUT THE AUTHOR

At the age of 26, ABEL KEOGH unexpectedly found himself a young widower. When he decided to starting dating again he looked in vain for resources that could help him guide him through the dating waters and open his heart to someone else. He found nothing. As he began blogging about his experiences, women dating widowers began emailing him asking for his thought on their situations. As the numbers of emails increased, Abel started writing a weekly dating a widower advice column. In *Dating a Widower* Abel shares the knowledge he's learned from his own experience and the most common issues he's seen from hundreds of emails from women dating widowers.

Abel is also the author of the memoir *Room for Two*— the story of the year of his life following his late wife's suicide—and the novel *The Third.* He and his wife Julianna are the parents of three boys and two girls. Learn more at www.abelkeogh.com.